Which Will Change the Other More?

poems by

Barbara Boches

Finishing Line Press
Georgetown, Kentucky

Which Will Change the Other More?

To Edward, Huan and Pang

Copyright © 2021 by Barbara Boches
ISBN 978-1-64662-655-7 First Edition
All rights reserved under International and Pan-American Copyright Conventions. No part of this book may be reproduced in any manner whatsoever without written permission from the publisher, except in the case of brief quotations embodied in critical articles and reviews.

ACKNOWLEDGMENTS

Thank you to the editors and judges who published the following in earlier versions of these poems:
Cha: An Asian Literary Journal: "Of Li Qing Zhao" and "Pantoum: In China"
HOOT Review: "Minimum Wage"
Ibbetson Street: "In The Assisted Living Center"
Poet Lore: "Summer Job, Florida"
Solstice: "The asylum seeker"
SWWIM Every Day: "Beatitudes of Sobrevivientes de Violencia Doméstica In ESOL Class"
upstreet: "The Heart in Chinese"
"Japanese Stewartia, Arnold Arboretum" appeared in the exhibition: "In Your Mother Tongue: A Word and Image Dialogue" Griffin Museum of Photography at the Lafayette City Center, Boston.
New England Poetry Club, Honorable Mention in 2020 Amy Lowell Prize: "To ESOL Instructors: For Their Safety—You Will Refer to Domestic Abuse Survivors by Flower Names"
New England Poetry Club, Honorable Mention in 2020 E. E. Cummings Prize: "Carolina Silverbell"

Many thanks to Roger Weingarten for his guidance and inspiration. Also thank you to Kathleen Aguero for years of advice and support on the majority of these poems, Sara Rivera and her GrubStreet workshop, Annie Finch, as well as Suzanne Berger and her workshop members encouraging me early on. I am indebted to Zhou Junwen for his teachings on Chinese language, history and poetry and to the beautiful ladies and survivors at the Women's Lunch Place and UU Urban Ministry who have educated me. Thank you to the Cambridge Community Center for the use of a photograph of their mural for my cover. These poems would not have existed without the support and enthusiasm of my husband, Edward, or without our children, Huan and Pang.

Publisher: Leah Huete de Maines
Editor: Christen Kincaid
Cover Art and Author Photo: Edward Boches
Cover Design: Elizabeth Maines McCleavy

Order online: www.finishinglinepress.com
also available on amazon.com

Author inquiries and mail orders:
Finishing Line Press
PO Box 1626
Georgetown, Kentucky 40324
USA

Table of Contents

To ESOL Instructors: For Their Safety—You Will Refer to Domestic Abuse Survivors by Flower Names 1
Caught 2
Before and After 4
Women's Shelter Xmas Eve Talent Show 5
Middle School New Girl 6
Field Trip Diptych 7
Teen Party, Halloween Storm 8
Snowman 9
An orange 10
Feathered Shoe. Yves Saint Laurent, 2004, The Met. 11
At the Park Avenue Armory 12
Times Headline: "Birds in China Fall to Lowest Level in Six Decades" 14
The Heart in Chinese 15
Morning Train to Chengdu 17
Ghost City Villanelle 18
Pantoum: In China, ...19
Of Li Qing Zhao 20
Monogamy 22
Cat and Dog 23
Carolina Silverbell 25
After the Pedi-Cab Ride 26
Japanese Stewartia, Arnold Arboretum 27
The asylum seeker 28
Beatitudes of Sobrevivientes de Violencia Doméstica in ESOL Class 30
Minimum Wage 31
Summer Job, Florida 32
In the Assisted Living Center, San Francisco 34
Notes 36

To ESOL Instructors: For Their Safety—You Will Refer to Domestic Abuse Survivors by Flower Names

Yarrow *oh, oh*'d in a basement
garden of sorts: fluorescence,
heat, dampness, rows

of growing things, where flowers might
linger a few hours to correct
lapses in the past, or perhaps practice

to be in present tense. That
class, bright, if rather bare, bordered
with laminate tables and folding chairs; a baby

slept in a stroller after lurching on subway
bus bus sidewalks ice
rutted down an elevator creaking

vowels, to where her
mother read: *I was in the jar* aloud, though
her book said *yard*. She

labored to learn *y* and remember
a plosive sound often followed
one liquid and soft. Still, that

garden burbled with lexical
hums murmurs, an occasional
laugh, and that afternoon, an instructor paraded

a tiered red white and blue
marvel for a break that wasn't
just a break but a celebration. Buddleia

stood first, salsa-d a bit in her snow
boots. Bee Balm belted: *Oh say
can you see*. Then Tulip put her thumb

and finger between two
lips and blew—the baby howled, flowers
whooped and clapped for the waking

and for Yarrow's citizenship and our
land that may one day blossom again.

Caught

up in the 90s by traders with stick pins, horse-
bit loafers, Thomas Pink
shirts, who bent toward numbers spinning

> now with those more valuable than the birds
> of the air who eat in a church
> basement, ladies who wheel nests

into futures
contracts—silk
purses for their glass towers. At night, we'd pile

> into a room with twelve moonlit beds. Others
> ascend to a library on three where carpet
> severs stone

into a dark, long
sedan to Nobu yellowtail and lychee
martinis. Once, we left to stumble,

> where ladies nap in four soft wing
> chairs. Left hand in flight—when confiding she's an international
> spy—now rests, tucked

in bitter wind, on to Le Cirque—when they learned I
had never been—and ordered suckling
pig untouched and bottles of Chateau

> near frosted glass that clouds
> Cartier, Valentino, and Armani shops. Another
> leafs through worn Maugham, sips

d'Yqeum. Outside, afterward, stood
a woman wrapped in a white
blanket. Snow landed lightly

> from a stashed
> flask, until she staggers
> up for help. sorry, so very

on the cup of cracked
blistered fingers I
pretended not to see.

Before and After

The beech branched into baldachin for
ladies leashed to golden

labs, lap dogs and Mt. Pleasant daily
dialogue, until a builder bought the shady

plot, subdivided its lot then chain
sawed the brocade of boughs. His

backhoe amputated below bark
laced knees then up

rose yet another big box. The ladies lamented
to zoning (who listened

politely) but between car
pools and pooch shots, they had to move

on. The beech, shrunken to a one
armed wild woman with spiked

brow, lingers, skirted
in boxwood, shod in sod—what

used to be fall's filigree
or summer's dark

damask holding out a last
handful of garnets.

Women's Shelter Xmas Eve Talent Show

Rita in rhinestone jeans is the first to fist-tap
her heart, shiver and swivel when *L'amour* trembles
off key but tenderly under dangling gold

garland. Then oval orange glasses hover over the mic: *I'm
a lesbi*an rhymes with baby bottle
gin, heroin, prostitution, prison, as *Um hm girl* echoes

through the caf. Next, a Sony on a steel
trolley bursts into *Santa
Claus is Coming* Karaoke. Bundled women at long empty

tables bounce up, air-box blue teardrop
baubles. All whoop until one whooper drops
three layers, hip-hops to *Let it Snow*. A knit

capped chorus stomps, crows *No, no.* Outside
a beaded curtain for no-snow
ladies to slip through when leaving; hail

ticks on sidewalks so
bewitching a sound I'll forget to mark shop
window mannequins pouting in Milanese red

knits, azure fur, azure boots. So
bewitching, I'll forget the treachery
beneath. But first Frosty, Rudolph and Chestnuts

Roasting. The felt-antlered chef closes with Maya
Angelou, as Rita—who once woke in Statler Park to a blade
of a man she bashed before she ran

to the ER—nods to *Phenomenal
woman, that's me*, finger-taps her
scar, shivering rhinestones.

Middle School New Girl

Sofia tapped the toe of a scuffed blue
pump: *They say you help with children.* Her kohled
eyes darted: *It's my daughter, hija.* Her face too

furrowed and leathered for a twelve
year old's mother: *First day, she go
to bathroom. Two boys go in too.* ESOL was beginning

across from the brick Nubian
Benevolent Society where they sowed
seeds for Allah as we dug into present and past

tense for our student survivors, sobrevivientes, 幸存者, while
warned not to unearth their pasts: *One with
a knife. They grab her.* But I was green, as was the shelter

worker who bum-steered her to me for a *school
issue.* My co-teacher patting
her Timex, clapped. We stepped

to the back, where coffee grinds and rancid
sponge wafted from a sink: *So she took
their knife and*—she swiped her pale frayed

sleeve with one finger—*boys run.* Her passion
pink nails clasped my wrist: *Now they
don't let her in school.* Dark ripple

of old burns crept out from her
cuff: *Knives, she know what to do*
and nodded. Soon

after, the shelter sent Sofia to a pro
bono lawyer and sent us other
mothers, students, survivors who sometimes

in tears or numbness or fright blurted: *Her
dad, papa,*爸爸, *do it to her. That's when
she first* sliced *her, su,* 她的 forearm.

Field Trip Diptych

> Suburban School Fourth Grade,
> Plimoth Plantation

So bored with talk of scythes
and salt, how many swine might
die by spring, Eliza prays, *Oh God,* for
a break, worms toward a Wampanoag
brave who weaves pink and yellow
strings on pins, *How
much*—Siri's her mother's Apple
Pay—cranes toward hands that
wind and waits. Painted
snakes on his brow
wriggle, his porcupine
crown starts to shake white
tail deer hair, whelk
beads. *Eliza!* swerves to
smile at teacher's crossed
arm glare, rolls
her eyes, shrugs, spins
away. Meanwhile, at the

> City School Third Grade
> The Children's Museum Bubble Room, Damon

dances off, comes
back with: *Why'd that lady shut
the door on me?* Shows he's not
read little labels explaining
things he sees cannot
be, things that make chaperones
debate: surface
tension might've fooled him. Distance,
dimness could've
confused him. Did she even
mean to? Damon stays where
teachers say, jerking
opals out of bins, brandishing
wands to billow
rainbows that
weaken, blacken, vanish, yet
obeys.

Teen Party, Halloween Storm

Blinded by bone-cold
snow, none trembled as she

left weaving, none called
her back from the squall, from

faltering into a white
bank, sinking into

it—edged in ice, clinging,
a fledgling in winter

covered gown before black
robed, plastic scythed, snow

booted, late to a party, Death slogged
by, stretched, then bent toward labored

breath, her vomit, and pulled
out his phone, waited on wailing

lights, as the mother who served
her shots, who laughing saw

her coatless, shoeless out
her door, wobbled

past bouncing beery ping
pong balls, up to drool

and snot on her downy
bed, as Death, alone, departed.

Snowman

This one hangs by a rope in the next
door oak, made of mesh, stuffed
with thistle to feed finch and chickadee, though he
attracts squirrels, which, to deter, our bird-
loving neighbors sat a black vinyl
slanting LP with red label halo
atop his top
hat. Rodents thump after they

slip down grooves of the British
band who would have known
birds as girls fluttering back
stage, snow as heroin, and squirrel as what
they didn't do with all they squandered
on birds and snow. I had a bird

friend once. Flamboyant, opposite
of most at our small
women's college, though she'd
often try to drag one of us to concerts
and parties, flitting
into our rooms in a red-lined black
satin cape, David Bowie 'do,
cajoling, then pouting when she
had to go alone. Drink, not drugs, more
her go-to—I remember her

drunk, laughing as she ripped
off her kimono to dance in thong and
pasties twirled into tiny batons. After the initial
shock, her exuberance spread, a scarlet
macaw stirring up wrens and sparrows. Out

my window, a gray squirrel starts
its slide followed by
free-fall and thud, replayed
and replayed, while up, high, the snowman grins,
swings, while the birds
flock to him still—whistling
and cheery-cheering.

An orange

parrot perched six
stories up: Frankie who, months
ago, settled on Emily's
sill for pizza crust and since
shredded her sweaters, and so separated
her from the more fastidious
of her friends. Off again, having chewed

her way out of her travel
case into strange currents that bore
her past Raspberry
Deli into a linden ringed by rusted
bike parts. Unreachable,
screeching, she wanted
out until she didn't—like my brother
in law who left town with Barnum. When
Frankie tried to fly, a southern
wind floated her to a rooftop

fence. My poor mother
in law; at 16 he'd already bashed
her car, flunked English and Wood
Shop. As the renegade called,
Emily raced through a propped
open door, six
flights up an unknown
stairwell while my future
husband sped his mother to Pawtucket to pick
up a sullen escapee who reeked
of Marlboros and elephant craps.

Feathered Shoe. Yves Saint Laurent, 2004, The Met.

Feathered crow black, but more
                      delicate, wind
swept, open
       toed. Chimney
swift, a raven dark

gust whirrs, curls, crests before swallow
         or sparrow cast themselves on five

lines strung across telephone
poles, charred

notes spaced in unequal
measures. If I could read
      music, I'd keen their
      lamentation: cormorant,

grackle. The subway
sign scrawled: capitalism +
      earth = ecological
      collapse. Three billion gone in the last

half-century. Cowbird, loon. The black
      stiletto, head
      on, poses toothless,
matted, still: in

profile, plumes praise all
urgency, all
flight.

At the Park Avenue Armory

Act 1. Her sucks on Her wine
red fingernail, rolls to kneel on white
wall-to-wall, bounces twice
on the bottom of a glass

box over a traverse
stage, straddles Her husband's lap
and whispers the inconceivable:
mid-career, she has found herself

in their first house to fill, and what
Her never had—never
having evolved from birth
control pills and condoms to *tick, tock,*

calendars and thermometers—she now has to
have. The clock in Her mirror
summons, its alarm over something just
beyond its reflection. In Act

2, Her maneuvers within a reversed
image until begetting must
begin with syringe and speculum, for when
did she and he not succeed, when did

science not. Her, who never
knew *no*, recites, *this
month*, and waits. In an empty
garden, she plants

a tree, impatiens, rue. Clomid,
Menopur, Bravelle, ART, IVF. In

centrifugation, she came
to trust—in goliath plastic

injectors: sperm, rinsed and spun
after synchronized days of reflection

over bathroom sink, needling
skin under white fire

retardant ceiling tiles taped
with *Nat Geo* orchid

and toucan, while coral
tipped toes froze

in stainless stirrups. Later, the gelled
wand above, *no*, a silk hat with no

scarves, no flowers or white
rabbit, Her disbelieves *no*

nothing that mattered
that she could not have, a body

always receptive to whatever she
asked of it *no* she slips

into a river she won't leave *no* ever
the same. Act

3. Cervix, a sieve, a sorrow: still,
who would follow caroming into limbic

rocks, whirled
into ecstasy, vodka, debauch. Husband turns

back as Her hurtles on, having to
have what a desert uterus won't. *no*

Hubris. Gods, emperors, pharaoh's
daughter have cradled blood

not theirs, but she, cocksure there's only
one way to mother, *no* sags against

glass, knifes Her
womb and sinks. Blackout. Don't
applaud.

Times Headline: "Birds in China Fall to Lowest Level in Six Decades"

At it again?—chasing with
nets, letting children out

of school to clang
pots and pans until the passerines drop

from exhaustion: to save grain
crops, which drumming families

did, until insects, locusts
multiplied. But, no, I blink. It's

births not birds. *Lowest
number since the Great

Famine*—which succeeded the sparrow
purge. Don't have one, have

two, China finally
has decreed, yet their millennials

don't. *Nobody wants to get
married…living

costs, time, energy…can't
think of a reason to have

one.* The last
visit to Beijing—with our two

China allowed us
to adopt—we watched them fly

kites above Tiananmen Square. Mid-
afternoon's gray haze, not
a bird in the sky.

The Heart in Chinese

The *heart* in Chinese is 心 ("sheen"
in a high flat tone) an ideogram
usually joined with

another, when the two, either set
side by side or over/under, will
take on new

meaning, *as spring's scents* 芳 join
the *heart* 心 to make a *young
woman's heart* 芳心 unfolding. Each

soft 柔 wing of the *tender
hearted* 柔心 without any
foreboding that love

drunk 醉 with
love can *obsess* 醉心 to
possess lilacs in blossom,

that the insistent *self* 己 can
bristle, *jealous* 忌 of
stigma and pistil—so

zealous as love shifts slowly
into *load* 担 to bow
in *worry* 担心 , and wind

stirs furious,
cold 寒。 *Disillusioned* 寒心
petals fall bruised, matted,

glued 贴。 The *intimate* 贴心
persists and twists, resisting
fears that

widen 宽 wanting
relief 宽心。 Fire grows
into ardor's

ash 灰。 Love, *discouraged* 灰心
and wracked with rue, *flees* 亡 to

forget 忘, until
spring returns, when the heart 心
whispers, "Make yourself

small 小。 *Be
careful* 小心。"

Morning Train to Chengdu

The local rocks stained
lacy curtains. The local rocks bungeed
baggage stowed above, rocks plastic
sacks with lychee nuts, jujubes crammed beneath

slat seats, rocks three
college girls who peek at us, then
American? The local doesn't get many English
speakers. We practice until I recite *California*

Dreamin' off one of their shirts, hum the old
pop tune about loving
California, which somehow makes them quiet
down and never speak

to us again. Even on the local, students must
practice caution with foreigners.
On the way down the aisle, sun
blazes through Qinling cliffs, on what's left

of a plank road, the sort
Li Bai warned was *harder than*
the sky to climb, then I squat
over a hole in the local's floor where railroad

ties flicker by. The bald conductor juggles pale
sand pears for squabbling
girls. I smile, *You should work*
with children, maybe

teach. Our young guide, sent to catch us up
to the tour group, translates. The conductor's grin
fades, as he murmurs before
retreating to his metal seat to stare

long at his tea over words the local boy doesn't
know not to repeat. *My life*
was chosen, all of us were once told
what to be.

Ghost City Villanelle

Thousand cranes sail—a city rising—
then bow to bamboo scaffolds around
steel skeletons that shutter

skies. Dots on the map, to our surprise, hold
high-rises that climb by tenfold. Thousand
cities for sale as cranes rise on tree

shorn roads. Abandoned rubble lies near new
doors festooned in red and gold. Under skeleton
shuttered skies, a grand

opening: a firecracker dragon writhing below
windows arrayed blank and colder than a thousand
cranes in a city that escalates enterprise. A women's

band in pink visors plies drums
and trumpets for new brick to behold
a sky that iron shutters skeletonize, towers so

much taller than Li Bai's, yet no
one to watch a distant sail on a river turning
gold. Thousand cranes scale skeletal
cities that cage ancient skies.

Pantoum: In China,

a poem flitted through a grove, misty and far
from the Emperor who forbid branches and leaves
near his own red walls and yellow roofs, except
in his private rockery. The Emperor who

forbid branches and leaves, likely to harbor
enemies, except in his
private rockery, shut
his eyes among its cypress and twisted stone. Unlikely

to harbor enemies, buried in his
guarded halls, walls, towers, he
shut his eyes among cypress and twisted
stone, fearing pain, 困, and trouble, 麻烦. Buried

in guarded imperial halls, walls, towers,
each brick and stone courtyard fifteen layers
deep, he so feared pain, 困, and trouble, 麻烦 inside
his gilded palace, he switched rooms every

night. Among brick and stone courtyards, fifteen
layers beneath silken quilts, behind pearl
inlaid screens inside his gilded palace, he switched
rooms every night, envying a poet's moonlit hut.

Beneath silken quilts, behind pearl
inlaid screens, within crimson walls and yellow
roofs, he envied the poet's moonlit poems flitting
through bamboo-striped mist.

Of Li Qing Zhao

To begin, she mused on her own
lips and hair, her powders

and pillows, gold
pins, silk screens, jade

flute, and the yearning when her
love travelled, a yearning that slipped

into stasis and sorrow when
widowhood, wanderings so

weighed and waited
on grief, she could not even

step into her skiff, certain
it wouldn't budge. Twenty-five years with her

husband-scholar, collecting bronze
horses, carved stones, until she fled

typhoid, war, South to where
Li Qing Zhao bends over a small

table, rubbing her shoulder, remembering
his fists, she who could best

any man or woman in words or games: fooled
into marrying again. Dismal, desperate, sick. Grey

light now touches the few scrolls not
burnt or stolen. So

kind at first, then like others, all
avarice. So she writes on her new

subject: Capture
the Horse, though her board and most

pieces lost. He never dreamt she'd suffer
prison to divorce. Frayed

robe, she brushes with bone
ink, *My whole life I've won most*

contests I have played. Rain
taps the wutong

trees, as she fingers her last jade
horse and, over her bitter
tea, smiles.

Monogamy

materialized mostly in
humans and gibbons, which manifested in extended

> *childhood and brain*
> *development for H. sapiens.* Chalk one

up for monogamy—bedrock in my Bible
Belt upbringing, so Dad astonished when he

> confessed he was *just*
> *a whippersnapper* when
> his dad *upped*
> *and moved out, took up*
> *with another a hunderd*

miles away. The lar gibbon is serially
monogamous, desertion occurring only if

> partners found parentally
> impaired or s/he encounters another with superior
> genes. *Granny could*
> *be difficult,* particularly after her oldest

passed. This
disclosure came to me late

> in his life; long married, past
> *my own livin' in sin* and his
> weeping over the phone: *didn't*
> *think you were that*
> *kind.*

Cat and Dog

When the house could no longer hold her son, when
clocks struck, and each minute, each second
sounded, second mother with him would run
to rutted roads near tidal beach—both beckoned
along by dog or crab—the cracks repaired
by black-topped ribbons on which they'd dance. He
grinned that, for a time, no one had cared
he led, and she: that he would let her balance
near him on strands, until they faced no black,
then commanding her to flap and *Fairyland!*
—they might pass. So they would track
past capes, blue hydrangeas and packed sand
until the hour demanded both go back
to what neither one could win nor end. Neither

could win nor end what, for each, was neither
game nor spat, but some essential
need for a mother and son to besiege.
She offered, he rebuffed, as if an existential
threat. Then ear by ear, hair by hair, each
disappeared. Their bouts played out in the kitchen
where blue willow plate cracked, as the peach
tree peeked at their disintegration
until, like gingham dog and calico cat,
not one tuft nor tooth was left. One ghost
remained to cook; another to combat
her: two who haunted the house until the host
packed up, parted from the peach tree at
the pane, and doomed the plate to a lone

post. Brooding over the pain of a lone
post, ghost dog fled along an asphalt track to
the mountains, cat to the coast,
where whisker, dewlap did come back,
and dog one day awoke to checkered fur,
while cat first licked the sand off spotted
pelt then scampered down the road in silver
light, to stumble on a stick dog that trotted
away as fast as he could from a mother
gray as ash, who pulled from oven
sweet breads and cakes. Afraid she loved him,

and what that meant, he shoved her
away to the Grimm tale again when
a mother's house could no longer hold him.

Carolina Silverbell

The first was for my first. The arborist
warned me against that

rocky ledge, but I wanted the newbie
where I could watch it

at daybreak. So it grew: soft
white bells the first spring, while the sapling

rooted, shallowly, its leaves dying
off even before she jiggered out

of the stroller in her powder blue
overalls to bolt. The second

for my second waved from the back—sheltered
by fir, settled in humus—until we left it one

hot summer. Alone, he charged off, past
pitch pines and beach roses to the razzle

dazzle of breakers on jetties. Many
mistakes. Yet, look, above winter

creeper and stone, the first
has come back, sturdier and nodding
its umbrella of blooms.

After the Pedi-Cab Ride

Outside the Beijing silk shop, it's
drizzling. A spinner in the alley winds
filament into thread, as cinnabar,
ceramics, painted bamboo and swallow scrolls, blue
willow tea sets, and Great Wall cigarillos draw
tourists to wood-framed
windows, while we huddle under red
umbrellas, near a parasol
tree, while the guide shouts about *mulberry leaves
and larva*. The spinner on the stone
stoop under tiled
eaves barely glances at Caucasian
parents with our Chinese-
born girls, though her fingers
freeze for a moment, while scarves
for sale flutter in the slightest

breeze. From the shop
door, a sharp call, rapid claps, as if to chase
off a pigeon or cat. The startled
spinner bends toward her bowl of boiled
cocoons. I wondered if these young
women who spin, paint, or polish
jade, if any had to give
up her daughter. I had met Li Quan who fled
to the States—family planning uniforms had
taken her month old because
she already had a son. One

tired girl tugs at her mother who murmurs
to wait. She wants to watch
the spinner swoop a nub into gossamer
sail, then reel, but
she won't, because the other daughters pull
away from the tree with its thousands
of shivering parasols.

Japanese Stewartia, Arnold Arboretum

A gardener wonders if she might
have done something long

ago for the one
thin in the shadow of his

brother, born on the wrong
side of rising storms and winds, as the thicker

stem bends from its own
kin. She did prune

wounds back to the collar, yet scars
yawn, and too little

sprouts while the other easily
branches and leafs. Could she

have gone farther, defying
nature's favoring, and trimmed

the stronger for the weak? Survival
of the fittest being the rule, and herself, not

one to scissor roots, wire branch, or
defoliate for aesthetics

sake, why, here, does she feel the need for more
symmetry? Perhaps if one

withers and drops
the other will be lost to fungus

and rot, when what she
wants is Hercules and young

Iolaus brandishing the torch, back
to back, facing the onslaught.

The asylum seeker

enters softly, her firm
step and swaying

hips, gone as she slips beside
me, whispering *God, please*

forgive me. Long fingers press
against eyelids. There, maybe, her children

flit. Did they
ever exist? I can't

help the thought. A wall between
us, though, through it, I glimpse

cracks in which flash
uniforms and fists. Two middle

aged women, we settle in a church
basement. I tutor

her. She sleeps
in a shelter. Our wall, only in part,

from different tongues. Other
bricks are mine. I don't want to

accept her tale, preferring
it to be a ruse—to gain

legal status. If only
a fraction's true—and this much is: she

was a prostitute (and had me
call her lawyer to hear the next)—then she

has lived hard enough, and if
all her lawyer added's real, if

the rest doesn't
belong to someone else, then how

does she wake, sleep, or speak
to God of her penance. One girl

taken. The other cut
from her uterus. I shudder as she

sobs, sinks from chair
to floor, her fist, like a silent
gavel, up and down.

Beatitudes Of Sobrevivientes de Violencia Doméstica in ESOL Class

Blessed is the fluorescence for those
long taught not
to speak, now learning
that ___*a* does not have to
refrain.   Blessed

is the pressed laminate, the long
tables lined with those
who once quailed before Cain, now learning
that *i* does not have to
lie silent.   Blessed

is the linoleum, the cork
dust beneath those
who used to kneel to keening, now
learning the silence of *e*
at the end of   refuge and escape.

Minimum Wage

If a tiny
chrysanthemum's slender

stalk and pistil could
arrange to wage a war, then it

might rage against the lack
of a living wage, so

often stemmed—Oh, if
it could win, then would we

behold bouquets of
daffodil and delphinium,

narcissus and allium no
longer going to

men of dominion to
frivol or squirrel.

Summer Job, Florida

The swelter started in the graveled parking lot, wobbled
over the Buick hoods before rolling

inside to pause at the great fans in the corrugated
metal arena, where stacked boxes

of doorknobs and men in white
short-sleeved shirts rode

forklifts singing *Jesus*, as if the surrounding
blaze was something for them to take

and make their own. With handkerchiefs
large enough to flag

surrender, they wiped
sweat as they stood at the window to the inner

sanctum, where women in blue rayon and miters of stiff
hair sat before black desks and a unit A/C that

dripped into a grey puddle, like the guilt of all
sinners, as they summed, subtracted, and kept

score in thick black books, ticking
off the multitude of the world's

evils and their need to ward off the devil who,
despite my upbringing, I had begun

to suspect was myth when, at Lord's
Hardware Supply Company during college

summers, I counted handles in the dusty
wilderness of Weslock

and Schlage. That August, I fell
from a ladder, hobbled into the office where men

and women gathered to lay
hands on my leg, their gibberish like snakes twisting

about my head. When they were
done with praise and prayer, when their happy

tears had subsided, I stood to their cheers and strode
straight, sore afraid, if I limped, I'd find
myself cast again into their fire.

In the Assisted Living Center, San Francisco

The bed cups Uncle into a broken
moon, a crescent of crepe
skin draping bones—vague
likeness to the soldier in the snapshot
he hands me, on a beach with Patton's
men who'd marched there from

Cherbourg. On my iPad, I play him
an aria from *Madama Butterfly*. Renata
Tebaldi: our favorite. *One
fine day, we will see...* His eyes
redden and close, "Nobody
aboard thinking of war." *The ship*

appears...the white ship... Ten
thousand on a carrier, but more like an island
of boys, he swore, climbing
hammock over hammock. He speaks
of sun & breeze, moonlight & men—an idyll
impossible to believe in

August after D-Day, but I nod because
we are a family that tucks discomfort
into drawers. Zuni
Café. Azure boa, red stilettos, pink
lamé. Transvestites samba past
our table. *Little wife, sweet*

*scent of verbena, the names
he called me...* Uncle leans over roast
something to murmur, "Sex isn't
important at my age." Unsure
what to say, I smile. Who
couldn't guess? *Out*

of the city crowds, a man... Yet,
even after he added
J's name to the deed and they
lived as man and man forty years, even after J
died and left everything
to Uncle, our family silently

folded, to stow away, what
had once swayed over a star
spangled ocean.

Notes

"An orange" was inspired by "The Day Frankie Flew Away" by Emily Flitter, *The New York Times*, February 19, 2020.

"At the Park Avenue Armory" Simon Stone's *Yerma* was loosely based on Lorca's play of the same name. Although he kept the title, he changed the main character's name to Her.

"Birds in China Fall to Lowest Level in Six Decades" includes quotations from "Births in China Fall to Lowest Level in Six Decades," by Sui-Lee Wee and Steven Lee Myers, *The New York Times*, January 17, 2020.

"The Heart in Chinese" Italicized words are the translations of the proximate Chinese character.

"Of Li Qing Zhao" This revision is based on Richard Egan's *The Burden of Female Talent: The Poet Li Qing Zhao and Her History in China* Cambridge, MA: Harvard Univ. Asia Center, 2014. Recent scholarship has acknowledged her second marriage, divorce and brief imprisonment in place of the traditional view of a suffering widow, which appeared in this poem's first publication. The quote is from Li Qing Zhao's "Preface to 'Capture the Horse', Diagrams and Text."

"Monogamy" Quoted material is from "Humans evolved monogamous relationships to stop men killing rivals" by Steve Connor, *The Independent*, July 29, 2013.

"In the Assisted Living Center" Italics are my translation from *Un Bel Di, Vedremo* in the libretto of Puccini's *Madama Butterfly*.

www.ingramcontent.com/pod-product-compliance
Lightning Source LLC
LaVergne TN
LVHW041559070426
835507LV00011B/1180